"Yes Is Forever!"

Mother Thecla Merlo
the first Daughter of St. Paul

ST. PAUL EDITIONS

NIHIL OBSTAT:
Rev. Richard V. Lawlor, S.J.

IMPRIMATUR:
+ Humberto Cardinal Medeiros
 Archbishop of Boston

Library of Congress Cataloging in Publication Data

Daughters of St. Paul.
 Yes is forever.

 SUMMARY: A biography of Mother Thecla Merlo the Italian nun who was a co-founder of the Daughters of St. Paul.
 1. Merlo, Thecla, 1894-1964—Juvenile literature.
2. Nuns—Italy—Biography—Juvenile literature. 3. Daughters of St. Paul—Biography—Juvenile literature. [1. Merlo, Thecla, 1894-1964. 2. Nuns. 3. Daughters of St. Paul—Biography.] I. Title.
BX4334.Z8D38   1979   271'.9 [B] [92] 79-22266

ISBN   0-8198-8700-5 cloth
       0-8198-8702-1 paper

Copyright © 1981, by the Daughters of St. Paul

Printed in the U.S.A. by the Daughters of St. Paul
50 St. Paul's Ave., Boston, MA 02130

The Daughters of St. Paul are an international congregation of religious women serving the Church with the communications media.

CONTENTS

The World of Mama Vincenza	13
The "Growing-Up" Days	17
Man With a Golden Dream	20
Decision	23
The Meeting	26
Teresa Meets a Man Named Paul	31
The "Miracle Newspaper"	34
Daughters of St. Paul	38
Feast Days Are Like a Mirror	43
The Walkers of God	47
How Does a Mustard Seed Grow?	53
Stamp of Approval	56
To Lands Across the Sea	61
A Time To Tremble	66
Gift in a Boxcar	70
Wartime Christmas	76
If Only a Package Could Talk	79
Do You Believe in Miracles?	83
Promises Must Be Kept	88
Growing Pains	92
She Gave All She Had	96
We Must All Be "Builders"	101
In the Footsteps of the Suffering Christ	104
Home...Beyond Those Stars	106

*Mother Thecla looked up at the dark sky;
her gaze roamed the heavens.
"There," she pointed, "there beyond those
stars is our Father's house;
the Father who is waiting for us.
How beautiful it must be to go home!"*

The World of Mama Vincenza

Mama Vincenza opened her eyes. It was morning, or was it really the middle of the night? As she wondered, not yet fully awake, the rooster in the backyard crowed. She glanced around and realized that her husband had already gone.

"Oh, Hector," she groaned to herself. "How long can you last working such long hours on the farm?" Tears sprang to her eyes as she thought of him while she washed and dressed.

Next to wake the children and tidy the house.

"John, it's time to get up for Mass.... Teresa...Costanzo...Charles."

As they walked along the dirt road, Mama breathed in the morning air and searched the Merlo farm for a trace of her husband. Sometimes she could see him leading the animals out of the barn or doing some other necessary chore. But not this morning. Eight-year-old Teresa slipped her hand into her mother's.

"I like to come to Mass with you, Mama, so that I can see Jesus in the white host, but I would like it much better if I could receive Him in my heart like you do."

"I know," the woman answered with a smile. She wrapped her arm around her daughter. "Just a few more months and you will make your First Holy Communion."

"Mama," she asked as they walked along, "what will it be like to receive Jesus in Holy Communion?"

"It will be like going to heaven," came the sure reply.

"Will I go to heaven soon?"

"Oh no, only after a lifetime of hard work."

"What kind of work? Sewing, cooking?"

"Perhaps, but the kind doesn't matter. What matters is to do what you can, the best way you can, for love of God."

The conversation continued until they arrived at the church and went inside.

* * * * * * * * * *

Castagnito is a small town in the northern part of Italy called the Piedmont Region. As the nineteenth century dawned, the people continued at the same steady pace—industrious, thrifty, unafraid of hard work. When 1899 slipped into 1900, they did not expect to suddenly become famous or rich. Life was simple. Each family built their home from raw materials provided by the Maker. They tilled the land and watched the crops begin to grow. They raised animals—chickens, cattle, sheep, pigs and horses. And the womenfolk spun cloth, fashioned it into clothes, cooked, baked, cleaned, mended and fixed. Yes, life was simple, and the people liked it that way.

Day after day the Merlo family walked to church. Mama Vincenza took the time and care to explain the "why's" of such a practice. She would

Teresa Merlo knew the love of a family that cherished one another.

never let them think that going to Mass was something they *had* to do. On cold days, all through the winter, she bundled them up and explained, as they walked, how sacrifice chosen for God's love builds strong citizens of earth and makes for a big reward in heaven.

"But," John asked once, "shouldn't I stay home and help Papa with the farm, at least in the summer?"

"Go to Mass first," Mama retorted. "You will work faster and better afterwards. Oh," she added, "if we only understood the value of the Mass."

The "Growing-Up" Days

Teresa added inches to her height and the years passed by. She received her First Communion, was confirmed, and to complete a well-rounded formation she was taught sewing and homemaking. Mama and Papa Merlo decided to send their daughter to the sewing school in Turin. That way, after a few months of intensive training she would return home a seamstress. It was worth the fee and even the sacrifice of her absence from home for the chance to learn such a useful trade.

The slender-built, serious teenager, with deep, dark eyes, filled her days with learning and activity. It never occurred to her that life could be anything different. She completed her schooling at Turin and returned filled with enthusiasm and energy. Now she wanted to convey to others what she had learned.

But there were times—at least once in a while—when her thoughts raced beyond her everyday life. "What if," she asked herself, as she stood staring at the grassy fields, "what if I could do more for God? I mean, the work could even be the same, but the dedication greater, like that of a sister?" She laughed to herself. "How silly. You think too much." She turned abruptly and went back into the house.

A few of the mothers on neighboring farms asked Mrs. Merlo if they could send their teenage daughters to Teresa for sewing lessons. Mother and daughter talked about it, agreed, worked out the schedule and the girls began to come. Teresa taught what she knew, explained as much as was necessary, repeated until it was clear for all. Then, she would do the work herself, making the demonstration practical.

But a class with Teresa Merlo meant more than just sewing. She had an appealing way of teaching what people call "virtues." Take, for example, the young girl who had a fine straw sewing basket, equipped with needles, thread, thimble, darning ball, etc. The lid had a mirror fastened inside. The girl would prop open the lid and watch herself, adjusting a curl, moving her face to one side and then another. Teresa noticed but did not say anything right away. She waited, then after more than a few classes she walked up quietly behind the girl, looked at her with a trace of a smile, and closed the lid. The girl's cheeks flushed. Teresa passed on without a word and continued the class in her normal tone of voice.

* * * * * * * * * *

The days were busy, but not busy enough to keep away thoughts about the future.... "My future," the twenty-one-year-old seamstress was thinking. "Do I want to continue as I am here? Or should I get married or..." the third choice left her perplexed. She had that "sister" feeling again.

"My Lord," she prayed with finality, "I will continue here as I am until You show me another road. Whatever it is, I want to do Your will."

Man With a Golden Dream

A war that would break the heart of a Pope, St. Pius X, a war so fierce and widespread as to be called the First World War, this was the situation of the year 1914.

While many boys were joining the army to advance the cause of justice, a young priest, spiritual director of the diocesan seminary of Alba, was recruiting an army, too. He talked of a most unusual way to preach the message of salvation. He was fired by the ideals of the spiritual giants of all time—men like St. Paul, St. Alphonsus Liguori, St. Bernard, St. Francis de Sales, St. John Bosco, St. Joseph Cottolengo and others who had met the needs of their hour with the methods and message of Christ.

He became convinced that the Church needed to Christianize the press apostolate, the printed word—newspapers, books, etc. But this priest saw into the future and realized that new avenues of communication were inevitable. What if the Church moved ahead with them? And why not? This was the need of the present century, the current "hour." Religious Congregations could be formed, whose members would be dedicated to

God's glory and man's salvation with the apostolate of evangelizing through the media.

"Who wishes to follow me?" This was the question Father Alberione asked. Some of the young men of his city of Alba listened in silence. "Follow you, Father?" they asked. "Where? To do what?"

What was Father Alberione's answer? "Come, join in my work. Come, give to the world Jesus, Way, Truth and Life. Come, be an apostle of the hour through the press and whatever new communication instruments the mind of man will invent." It took a lot of faith, much more than their youthful imaginations could paint. They didn't exactly understand the mission but one thing was clear—the steady, humble gaze of Father Alberione. He was confident, serene, as though the sole possessor of some wonderful secret.

A small man, slight of build, Father Alberione had been raised in the northern part of Italy. His appearance was nothing more than ordinary, yet everyone could see that there was something special about him. After a talk with him, they were convinced that he possessed a vision as wide as the world.

"We must teach all nations," he would say. "Think of the 4/5 of humanity who do not yet know Christ. Who will bring them the message of salvation? This must be our constant preoccupation." The dynamic priest dreamed of forming a

Congregation of modern apostles who would write, illustrate, print, bind, and diffuse the priceless message of salvation to a world hungering for God.

Young men began to join Father Alberione, and the year 1914 moved ahead. The war was mushrooming and breeding endless misery. Father Alberione's army was mushrooming, too. His boys had taken over their first printing shop. They called it a typography school. The priest instilled in his apostles the motives and the spiritual nourishment they needed to sustain them against all the temptations that the world dangled in front of their youthful eyes.

"What would St. Paul do if he were in our place? He would man your printing machine," the priest said, pointing to the boys working it. "He would set the type, print the pages, turn those pages into books, and then take the word of God to the people of today. We must be the 'Pauls' of our century."

They listened wide-eyed, those first followers of Father Alberione, and proved by their hard work the good will involved.

What would become of it all? Father Alberione—"the theologian" people called him—was fully aware of the countless eyes that watched. What were they thinking? What did it matter? "If our goal is from men then it will fall by itself," the priest whispered as he walked to the chapel, "but, if it is from God, who can stop it?"

Decision

Standing with both hands in his pockets, Costanzo Merlo looked out of the window. A mental battle was raging. The priest, Father Alberione, was the topic of the young seminarian's debate. "I want to help him," he mumbled. "I want to support his wonderful work, yet I feel that my call is here as a diocesan priest. Why, then, am I so mixed up?"

A hand clasped his shoulder. The young man turned around and met the gaze of Father Alberione.

"Costanzo," the priest said, "I would like you to do me a favor."

"Sure," he said, not knowing what to expect.

"I have heard nothing but good about your sister, Teresa. She has a fine character, leadership qualities, and a thorough home formation. Would you ask your mother to let her come to Alba to teach sewing to the young girls who will be future religious?"

"Well, I'll ask, Father," the boy answered, but there was a slight hesitation in his voice. He was thinking of Mama. Would she ever consent? Costanzo tried to be enthusiastic and yet *realistic* at the same time.

"Father, it might take a little while to convince Mama, but I'll do my best. Teresa will come; I know she will. Anyway..." the boy added as an afterthought, "it's not that she will go forever; probably just a few weeks until the girls learn their skill."

The priest smiled, "Now, Costanzo, you do your part and leave the time limit up to God."

* * * * * * * * * * *

"No, no,...Costanzo. I don't want Teresa to go." Mama's eyes were troubled. "Father Alberione does not need her. There are plenty of seamstresses in Alba."

Costanzo had expected that answer, and he was ready:

"But they don't have the good qualities and Teresa is only twenty-one. She has a lifetime of energies to give to God."

"A lifetime, Costanzo? But, you said only two weeks!"

"Oh, Mama," the boy said quietly. "O.K. for now."

Two weeks passed by. Costanzo tossed the problem back and forth in his mind. He couldn't let Father Alberione down, not a priest like that. He deserved support and help.

Teresa watched the dilemma from the sidelines. She had been doing a lot of thinking. Was this what God wanted of her—to join in the work of Father Alberione? From what Costanzo had said, the priest was really a man of God. If there was something, anything at all, that she could contribute, then she would do it.

"Once you told me when I was very small,..." the young woman squeezed her mother's hand, "that 'it doesn't matter what you do in life; it matters that you do God's will.' "

Her mother's eyes filled with tears.

"Mama," Teresa added gently, "I feel that this is God's will. Let us go to Alba and see what Father Alberione wants me to do."

The Meeting

Mama Vincenza kept her worries to herself. "After all," she thought, "children do grow up. If this is all in the plan of God, what can I say? Besides, Teresa hasn't even talked to the priest yet. She might decide against the whole idea. Oh dear," Mama sighed, "there is something so final about it all."

Mother and daughter walked the two hour journey to Alba. Teresa matched her steps with her mother's as they said the rosary aloud. Then they talked and Mama lamented about John, her oldest son, who had gone to fight in the war. He had been in the front lines for months.

"Don't leave me, too," the woman whispered.

"I will never leave you, Mama," Teresa said with a smile. "In spirit we will always be together."

They walked through the front door of St. Damien's.

"You wait in the pew here, Teresa. Say some prayers," Mama said. "I will go to find the priest."

The girl knelt. She tried to pray, but her imagination kept running away with her. "Why is Mama taking so long?" she asked nervously, as the beads of her rosary slipped through her fingers. Then, there were footsteps coming up the side

THE MEETING

aisle, closer and closer. The girl turned. Mama was straight-faced but serene.

"Father wants to talk to you. He is in the sacristy."

Teresa genuflected, walked quickly to the front of the church and entered the small room next to the main altar. There she found a priest—short, thin, humble. They talked; the meeting was brief. A few minutes later the girl was back in the pew with her mother.

Mama Vincenza kept glancing sideways at her daughter. Finally she could wait no longer. They left the church and she asked: "What did Father say to you?" They were walking again the familiar road back home.

"He asked me to help with his work," Teresa replied.

"What work?" asked Mama.

"Father says that women can do much good with the press, the printed word."

"But," asked the woman, "what does that have to do with you? What are you to do?"

"Nothing," the girl said simply, "just obey him."

There was silence. Then Mama Vincenza asked: "What answer did you give?"

Teresa was radiant as she replied: "I said 'yes.' "

Neighbors questioned the Merlo family. "How can you let your daughter get involved in a venture that is so uncertain?"

"There are many fine orders of sisters in the Church," said others. "She will have much better opportunities if...."

Hector Merlo was mild by nature, industrious and quiet. Everyone knew that it took a powerful wind to get him upset. But one thing that angered him when little else would was people who minded other people's business. "It's her life," he said. "As long as she does good, whatever she does, Mama and I will back her up." Teresa overheard the episode, smiled to herself, and then slipped out of sight so Papa would never know.

The girl packed her clothes, the necessary things, and was on her way. To do what? Right now *it* could best be called the will of God.

"In a few short weeks the girls will know how to sew and you will be home," said Mama, almost as though she believed it. Teresa tried to smile.

"I'll be counting on your prayers, Mama and Papa. Like you've always said, 'everything depends on prayer.'"

Mr. Merlo pulled out his big cotton handkerchief and blew his nose.

"I never cried in my life," he growled, trying to be stern, "and I'm not going to start now."

Teresa kissed them both; the parting was hard. As the horse and buggy jostled along, the future Mother Thecla Merlo looked out the window. Whatever her eyes pictured, her mind turned

As they walked the familiar road back home,
Mama asked many questions.

into meditation. She scanned the crops that soaked in the hot June sun. "Next year new crops, and the next year, and the next." She was lost in thought. "This life is a perpetual beginning anew. Always a new challenge, another victory to win. How senseless would everything be without heaven, without eternal life. Life with God is life without change, without end."

Teresa Meets a Man Named Paul

It was as if she had always been there. Teresa blended right in with the group of Father Alberione's apostles. She joined in their prayer, their work for God, which, during those first days meant sewing shirts so badly needed by the soldiers fighting in World War I. She joined the young women who were as dedicated as sisters but who as yet were not religious. She grasped their desire to become teachers to the whole world through the printed word. If people had only known, how they would have laughed. The matter was amusing by human standards but Father Alberione's band was not marching under a "human" banner. For them everything was in the hands of God and His Mother. But they had another heavenly helper too—the apostle Paul.

"What would St. Paul do," spoke Father Alberione, "if he returned to our world today? It has been suggested that he would be a journalist. I agree.

"Paul of Tarsus, the apostle who moved like a flame through city after city, kept in touch with his converts of the early Church by means of his letters. His written messages were carried to Corinth, to Philippi, to Ephesus, etc. The Christians gathered together and listened to those letters time and again. They made copies, circulated them, and then gathered them back again. Years passed. Christianity survived bloody persecutions and slowly sunk its roots into the mighty Roman Empire. Then barbarian hordes overran the world-power that long before had ruined itself from within. But all was not lost.

"In great stone monasteries, silent dedicated men wrote with feather pen on scrolls. Hour after hour they copied the words and paragraphs of holy Scripture, God's letter to mankind, including, of course, the Letters of St. Paul. How much good those words have done.

"Eventually, hand-written pages were formed into books, carefully bound with durable covers. Yet, how few were these until a man named Gutenberg invented a printing machine that could do what the swiftest pen in the world could not do. Down through the years, methods were perfected. Today the press apostle can preach to untold numbers with a single printing machine."

Teresa Merlo reflected: "Here I am dreaming of being an apostle of the press and I've never even seen a printing machine." She chuckled to herself and then reflected: "We need a father and protector. How good it is to have St. Paul on our side. He is really the master of our house. Somehow he will make up for all that we lack."

Teresa had decided to stay, to give her energies for a lifetime to this new apostolate. Everything would take time, prayer and sacrifice, and all would come true with the faith and guidance of their priest-founder.

December 8, 1917 saw the end of a war.

The sewing machines were silent now, but Teresa Merlo and her companions were not without work. They taught catechism to youngsters while they themselves attended theology classes conducted by Father Alberione.

The "Miracle Newspaper"

Father Alberione knocked sharply on the front door. Teresa answered. The priest took off his hat and began to speak. "Teresa," he said, his voice quiet and calm, "have you ever been to Susa?"

"No, Father," came the reply. "Why do you ask?"

"Bishop Castelli has asked me if you and your companions will take charge of his diocesan newspaper."

Teresa grew shaky and weak. Why, this was the chance of chances, but how? Where would they get the training and skill? She groped for words that would not come. The priest found words quickly: "Shall I accept for you?" he asked.

"Father," she responded with dismay, "you know we are few; you know, too, what we are capable of doing. Only Emilia is able to set type, and not very well. How are we going to do it?"

"Come to our typography for a few days. The seminarians will teach you. And do not forget that our Lord, His Mother, and St. Paul will help."

"Yes, Father," she said with a strong, clear voice. "Yes, we will come."

After a brief period of training, the young women prepared to leave for Susa where they would, with God's help, be printing the diocesan newspaper. The trip to Susa was brief and uneventful. The young women hardly looked at the city sights. They wanted to see their first printing plant, to inspect the unusual machines and to apply their newly-acquired techniques. They walked through the front door of the old house without a word. Eyes scanned the dust-covered equipment. The group knelt down. Teresa began an Our Father, Hail Mary and Glory Be to the Father. There was a moment of silence and then all became activity. Someone grabbed a broom; another found a pail, soap and scrub brush. Another dusted away the cobwebs.

Fifteen days later their first issue of "Valsuza" was shipped out to the readers. They hardly believed it themselves. A letter arrived from Father Chiesa, a great supporter of the infant Congregation. Teresa read it to the community while they were at supper.

"My good daughters, wonderful! Very well done! I received the first issue of 'Valsuza.' It was excellent. Who would distinguish it from any other newspaper for the way it is printed? One can see that the blessings of God are with you. See how fortunate you are: in the twinkling of an eye, you have ascended the pulpit to teach an entire diocese.

"What preacher in Susa has an audience as large as yours? You are sending the good news to everyone."

Time passed—weeks and months were filled with many new experiences in writing, printing, diffusion. They opened a small book center and took on additional studies needed for the apostolate, working as they studied. Some years later they returned to Alba where their work expanded and continued to develop.

The pioneer Sisters were called to bring Christ to the world
—in the spirit of the evangelizer Paul—
through the printed word.

Daughters of St. Paul

Seven years passed by. Father Alberione's group of young women had proved their will power and constancy of purpose. It was time for them to take another step. They wanted to be more than a dedicated team; they wanted to be religious sisters. Father Alberione instructed them on the essentials of religious life.

"Religious life is the 'following of Christ,' " he began, "but how, in our everyday living, can we do this? First of all, with the vows of poverty, chastity and obedience."

These three vows, or sacred promises, bind a religious closely to Jesus. With the vow of poverty, the sister chooses to do without extra things that she does not really need, and to work hard in her very special apostolate. By the vow of chastity she promises to think and be pure, and to give her heart totally to Jesus. By the vow of obedience the sister gives Jesus her will, and obeys her superior whom she knows represents God. These vows make religious life very special and precious to God.

Father Alberione explained: "When God creates a soul, He prepares it for a particular mission; He arranges everything and gives everyone qualities for the present and for the future, in such a way that each can attain that determined degree of eternal glory in heaven.

"Everything has already been foreseen in the mind of God. In creation, therefore, the Lord gives those natural qualities of intelligence, tendencies and health that each person will need for his or her vocation.

"The Lord disposes the parents the child will have and the surroundings in which he will live. Yes, the Lord disposed everything before creating our souls; He prepared the family, the parish, the schools and the environment according to His designs.

"A vocation, then, is not born in a heart at ten or fifteen years, but at the beginning of life when the Lord created the soul. The vocation comes from the heavenly Father and every infant who is born has his own vocation, his own destiny."

July 22, 1922—the weather was hot as the young girls took turns stepping to the altar rail and kneeling down.

"I, Sister Teresa Merlo," spoke the first, "in honor of the most Holy Trinity, of Mary, Queen of the Apostles and St. Paul, Apostle, for the greater glory of God and that of my neighbor, with the help of divine grace, offer, give, and consecrate myself to God with the vows of poverty, chastity and obedience."

The next sister stepped forward, and the next, and the next. It was the first public profession of the faithful group. Now they were religious sisters, bound to Jesus for a lifetime. Father Alberione inquired among them about their choice of a superior. Would Teresa Merlo be the best? He had prayed earnestly to know. He approached each sister, individually, and asked her opinion. Everyone agreed. He took the decision to the only one who didn't already know.

"I have thought it well to appoint a superior of our small Congregation," spoke the Founder.

"Oh, yes," Teresa Merlo, now Sister Thecla, agreed. "A good superior is essential for our spiritual growth."

The priest nodded his head. "You are absolutely right." He hesitated a moment. "The choice has been decided," he said softly.

"Fine," Sister said good-naturedly. "I will obey whomever you wish. Who is the new superior, Father?"

"You," he replied. Sister Thecla stared at Father Alberione. Her dark eyes reflected her concern. "But, it is not..., but it *must* be a mistake."

"Instead," interrupted the priest, "it *must* be God's will." He put on his hat and walked to the door of the convent.

"Have courage.... This is God's work, not our own. With Him we can do all things."

Sister Teresa pronounced her vows on July 22, 1922. She would now be called Sister Thecla.

Mother Thecla needed advice. She went to a priest whose holiness and sound judgment were well-known. "Father Chiesa," she said with apparent calmness, "Father Alberione has given me too much responsibility and I am not at all capable." She expected the priest to agree, to speak up in her defense, but he replied simply, "You do not have to do anything. You only have to obey and to believe. And you will see."

* * * * * * * * *

The Congregation needed a name. These women were called to be the St. Pauls of the modern era. Should they be called "Sisters of St. Paul?" The title was close, but not good enough. They were the little ones, the children of such a mighty protector! Dare they think they represented him as his religious or should they instead hope to be his humble children, his daughters? The Founder pondered and prayed, his usual custom, and came up with the Congregation's name. *Daughters of St. Paul* they would be.

Feast Days Are Like a Mirror

Every time someone called her by her new name, Mother Thecla seemed to hear the words of the Founder given in a sermon:

"The superior is to be a model of religious observance: in community life, in poverty, in work, in the spirit of sacrifice, at table, at rest, in the apostolate, in clothing, in furnishings."

It was all so new to Mother Thecla. Sometimes she felt like a fish floundering on dry land. Every day, every minute of the day, she was at her post, directing the community, solving new problems, groping for solutions, working to acquire in her own life the virtues expected of a religious.

"You are to be perfect," Jesus had said, "even as your heavenly Father is perfect" (Mt. 5:48).

"How long will it take?" the young Mother General felt like asking our Lord. But maybe it was better that she didn't ask. The answer might have been too much all at once. No doubt He would have said: "A lifetime, Sister Thecla, until the very last breath of your earthly existence."

She knelt alone to make her daily hour of adoration.

"Dear Jesus," she prayed, "our community is so small. How can we ever become what You expect? When will I be able to see with the faith of Father Alberione?" Without realizing it she stretched her arms toward the tabernacle and continued. "Show me what I can do to help us become the kind and number of Daughters of St. Paul that our Founder expects. No amount of knowledge and skill can buy the faith that makes miracles. Only You can give that faith, Jesus, here at the tabernacle. Make up for all that I lack...help me to do more and better...for You."

She left the chapel, put her books on the shelf and glanced out of the window. Storm clouds were piling up. The community bell rang throughout the convent; it was supper time. Mother Thecla fingered her rosary as she walked to the refectory where the community had gathered. Each stood at her own place, in silence. "In the name of the Father, and of the Son, and of the Holy Spirit," began Mother Thecla. "Bless us, O Lord...,"—the community joined in—"and the food we are about to receive to keep us in Your holy service."

The sisters sat down. "Is no one reading tonight?" she asked softly.

"Not tonight, if you think well," the sister next to her whispered. "It's your feast day, and...."

"Oh," exclaimed Mother Thecla, good-naturedly. "How could I have forgotten my own feast day? Is that good enough reason to dispense of the customary silence for the first part of the meal?"

"Yes," the sisters chorused. And someone added, "We have written a song just for the occasion." They rose and gathered informally to sing their home-style tribute to Mother Thecla.

The song continued—daughters' tribute to a mother—young though she was, for her total donation of self to their Congregation. They pledged obedience, fidelity to the cause of the Pauline way of life and sang of the day, not too far away, when with God's help, the Daughters of St. Paul would take the Gospel to all the nations of the earth.

Mother Thecla stared at the hand-written copy of the song being sung. She examined each line, meditated the words, and her thoughts went back to the chapel, to her conversation with Jesus just before supper.

"I prayed for faith, I begged You for faith, my Jesus. And You have given it. You have spread it around to these good sisters. Numbers mean little. If we are united, if we are zealous and obedient to Father Alberione, the world is ours."

The song ended. Mother Thecla rose from her chair and folded her hands at her waist. She smiled and tilted her head the way she did when she was pleased about something.

"Your song is a meditation," she said softly. "I treasure it very much. And there is no better time than St. Thecla's day to apologize to you all for the many times I was of bad example, for the offenses I might have given you. I ask pardon to each of you personally if I have ever caused you to suffer in any way."

The sisters glanced at each other in shocked surprise. "Where did this come from?" asked one. "Stop," whispered one of the older sisters with a smile. "You don't want to ruin our party."

The Mother General sat down. Her troubled face grew calm and she began to smile. Mother Thecla treasured these moments that foster the serene family living of which she was to speak so often. She loved to be with the sisters, to share not only prayer and work, but also hobbies, stories of apostolic adventures, songs, and even problems. This is what made her so special. Then the sisters sang the song again.

The Walkers of God

Mother Thecla was in chapel again. There was something definitely on her mind, and she was praying for the grace not only to understand it herself but to explain it to the sisters. Actually, it was about an inspiration of the Founder, an inspiration and an *invitation* to begin another apostolic initiative.

"I have realized for quite some time," the priest said to Mother Thecla, "that we can write books, many good books, and pile them neatly into the storage room. But that is only part of the work of the apostle. Our mission can never be complete until the word of God is in the hands of people. How many will come to us? Maybe ten percent? And what about the other ninety percent of mankind? *We must go to them.*"

This marked the beginning of a wonderful new aspect of the Pauline apostolate—taking the word of God directly to the people.

"We must have a great mind, a great heart," spoke Mother Thecla to the sisters. "Think of the whole world, of the many souls to be saved, of the many who await the light of the Gospel.

"Be concerned about the glory of God, about becoming good, about doing good to souls, and all the rest will be given to you by God. We will offer a beautiful homage to God, to the most holy Trinity, who wants to enter into those hearts, into those souls, who wants them saved. Let us be generous. God will not be outdone in generosity: the more we give, the more He will give us. To be an apostle, to care about the souls of men, that is what gives joy and vigor to a religious. For when she is concerned about the eternal welfare of others, her own small aches and pains shrink to their proper size. *We* want to be apostles," the young Mother General continued, "and what better way than to perform the same mission as the twelve apostles—to go, two by two, to every person and bring the good news of salvation?"

The sisters rejoiced at this new and direct approach. With the few titles available they made packages that were of carrying size, and set out. The torrid heat of summer beat down on their sturdy shoulders and perspiration streaked their faces, as they went on foot to the towns assigned them.

Imagine the reactions—varied and interesting—as the good-hearted farm people saw young women crossing their fields with an armful of books. If for no other reason, curiosity alone made people open their doors in a gesture of welcome.

"Who are you? What do you do? Well, well! I can't believe it. I just can't believe it." Slowly but surely Pauline books, made with struggle and sacrifice, found their way into homes.

The youthful apostles learned many things in their day-to-day contact with people. They found the hidden joys known only to those who give themselves willingly to the work of the Father, a joy shared with Jesus the Worker. They learned how to pray to Someone much more powerful than themselves, to the only One who can move the minds and hearts of men. They learned how to struggle against momentary obstacles, to make decisions, to plod on and keep up enthusiasm, to strive for constant self-improvement, both personal and apostolic. Those young women attended the school that majored in faith and holiness. Book after book left their hands and stayed with the people they met. Then back home, in the silence of the chapel, the sisters prayed for all those whom their lives had touched that day. It soon became obvious that this form of diffusion was essential to their Pauline apostolate. It was here to stay.

Father Alberione told the sisters: "Rich in merit and very effective is the personal diffusion of the word of God. It means going through towns and regions, going from house to house, in city and country, in valleys and on mountains, without any preferences, without any distinctions: it means to go to souls."

Mother Paula Cordero, many years later, would tell the postulants, novices and professed sisters of the American province how she, as a postulant, had gone out for an entire day to dif-

Two by two, the Sister-apostles began to diffuse God's Word to individual families.

The first Pauline bookcenter ▶

fuse God's word with Mother Thecla. "We visited the good, hard-working farm families," recalls Mother Paula, "and I remember so clearly that Mother General insisted that I not tell anyone who she was. I obeyed, and we enjoyed ourselves to see the books appreciated. We talked about our joy and prayed for each family as we walked from farmhouse to farmhouse."

How Does a Mustard Seed Grow?

It was the most unique room of its day, the "furniture" being two printing presses, a folder and a cutting machine. All the type-setting was done by hand. Somehow sheets of paper were turned into bound books. The process was slow and the finished product meager. How would they ever be able to supply the whole world with their message? Father Alberione had been thinking much about that. He spent extra time in prayer, searching for the answer that he knew would come if he had faith enough and patience enough to wait. Sometimes he meditated on the map of the world and seemed to see the anxious faces of men looking to him and saying: "Bring us Christ. Bring us Jesus as St. Paul did to the early Church."

Mother Thecla watched with awe as the Founder seemed to reach new heights of union with God. She coined a phrase of her own. "I put faith in his faith," she would tell Jesus in the tabernacle. "Do not look at my weakness, but see only the faith of Father Alberione. He thinks of new ideas for the apostolate that I cannot imagine and yet they come true. Have patience with me, and help me to cooperate totally."

"Our Pauline Congregation is like a river," explained Father Alberione. "A river becomes larger as it flows on because of the rain, the melting of the ice and the streams that flow into it. The waters thus gathered are then divided and channeled to irrigate the fertile plains. They will soon flow to various nations to benefit many. And then, some day the channels of water will reunite to empty into the sea of a happy eternity in God." To the sisters who listened in the tiny chapel the words were prophetic. But one phrase haunted Mother Thecla. Over and over she heard that sure voice of the Founder uttering words that made her faith shiver: "The waters will soon flow to various nations...." What could it mean?

The young Congregation had already begun to grow. January 19, 1926 saw the opening of a small convent in Rome. Much prayer, much hidden sacrifice earned *this big step* for the first Daughters of St. Paul. Once they had hardly thought of leaving Alba, at least not for a long time, but now they would go to one Italian city after another: Cagliari, Verona, Bari, Napoli, Salerno, Treviso, Palermo, Genoa, Reggio Emilia, Eldine—and all in a span of three short years.

God was with them. The fact became more and more obvious. But Mother Thecla guarded closely the humility of her sisters. "Sometimes we rejoice," she once said. "We say this has been done; that has been accomplished. But who did it? Our Lord did it. If there is something good, it is from God. Someone might say: You Paulines are beginning to do many things. What do we do? In the Gospel Christ said: 'When you have done everything that was commanded you, say, We are are unprofitable servants.'

"We must grind this basic truth into our hearts, Sisters. What are we capable of doing by ourselves? Nothing. By ourselves we can do nothing, but with God we can do everything."

The sisters were young; youthful enthusiasm ran high. There was an eagerness to support every project and a willingness to believe the words of Father Alberione and Mother Thecla. They worked with an energy far beyond their years.

There were so many ways to spur oneself on to new fervor. In the press room one sister called out the mysteries of the rosary and said "Hail Mary, full of grace...," while the other sisters answered, "Holy Mary, Mother of God...." Then, throughout the day, ejaculations rang back and forth. "Jesus, meek and humble of heart..." called one. "Make my heart like unto Thine," came the answer in chorus. But the favorite was: "O Saint Paul the Apostle our patron, pray for us and for the apostolate of the editions."

Dedication, enthusiasm—these furnish the spirit that no amount of money can buy. An army of one hundred thousand, without these ingredients, can be crushed; but a team of twenty or so, united in the love of God, can conquer the world.

Stamp of Approval

"Oh, if only we could print sisters as we print books," Mother Thecla said as she walked through the hallway into the refectory. The growing community awaited her there. Everyone had heard her familiar quick step and they were smiling as she walked through the door. It was early fall. After the grace before meals and a short spiritual reading, conversation began and someone mentioned heaven. Mother Thecla listened attentively. Heaven was one of her favorite topics. A glow stemming from conviction seemed to light her face.

"Life is a ship," she said thoughtfully. "Yes, we are sailors on a long, treacherous voyage. But, just as the sailor arriving in port no longer remembers the tiresome and dangerous days spent at sea, so will it be for us when we reach the port of eternity. We won't remember the struggles of our yesterdays; so let us never be stopped by sacrifices, but rather, work constantly for heaven."

And *work* was a word very familiar to the Daughters of St. Paul. They learned quickly that lofty goals take effort, the disposition to be of constant service, and a generous *"yes"* to Christ.

For quite some time a wonderful rumor had woven its way in and out of the sisters' conversations. It was the talk of receiving a religious habit. The reason? To give them a modest and distinctive mark of their total consecration to Christ. The Founder had expressed his wish, and Mother Thecla, with a few of the sisters, designed the dress. That was the first and most difficult stage. But the design had not remained just on paper.

The sisters who ran the printing presses, the machine that folds the printed pages into books, the cutting machine, and those who performed other duties by day, worked quietly into more than a few nights after the rest of the community had gone to bed. They were cutting, basting and sewing the first religious habits of the young Congregation. Mother Thecla enjoyed herself in the midst of the happy group. As her hands moved swiftly, guiding the needle to its proper end, her mind drifted back to Castagnito, to Mama Vincenza. How much time they had spent—just the two of them—talking and working, sharing the sweet moments that a daughter never forgets.

"How important to have that family spirit in a community of religious," she thought to herself. She shared this conviction with her sisters. "Love everyone without exception," she told them. "If we love each other we will make swift progress toward sanctity. It takes mutual charity to achieve a happy family atmosphere. Let us treat each other well, with respect and cordiality, rejoicing with our sisters who rejoice, and sympathizing with those who suffer."

October 28, 1928—The trees and hills were stunning, but for the sisters the dominant color was "black." There was not a tinge of mourning though. In fact, all was joy, for black meant that the day of religious investiture had finally arrived.

Those who, several years before, had been the first to profess their vows, plus the newer members who were old enough, walked in line up the aisle to the altar rail. The ceremony was solemn yet simple. Father Alberione blessed the folded habits and handed one to each sister. Each kissed the coveted gift and carried it out of chapel. They removed forever the plain dresses they had worn until then, and returned wearing the religious habit of the Daughters of St. Paul.

Slowly, but very surely, the die was being cast—the die that would cut and mold the spiritual identity of a twentieth-century Order in the Church. Sisters with a specific goal, a two-fold purpose: "Be perfect as your heavenly Father is perfect," and, "Go, teach the whole world." The Pauline way would be the powerful communications media: the press, radio, motion pictures and television. With Christ as her ideal, and Mary as her model, spurred on by the zeal of Paul, the Daughter of St. Paul would be ready to give Christ to the men of today.

On October 28, 1928, the pioneer Daughters of St. Paul received the religious habit.

Was it all too far-fetched? "Doubters" there would always be, but who could break the faithful determination of Father Alberione and Mother Thecla?

Diocesan approval of the infant Congregation was obtained in 1929.

To Lands Across the Sea

The sunlight began to linger on a bit longer and the greyness of winter was replaced with patches of green. Sister Paula, who would be one of the pioneer missionaries to America, spent full days making books with the eternal message, and other days taking the finished product to the people. All the while she prayed and hoped to carry the Pauline life to mission lands. But she never mentioned a word of this to anyone. Extra prayers, extra mortifications won the grace she sought.

She climbed the stairs to the first landing, carrying a pile of clothes. Mother Thecla called from the bottom step. "Sister Paula, come down for a minute." Her voice had a happy ring. "Have you been praying for a special grace?"

"Oh, yes," sister replied.

"I thought so," Mother Thecla said, "and as far as I am concerned, God has said 'yes.'" Sister Paula's face glowed as her superior continued. "I have chosen you to go to a special country."

"Brazil?" asked Sister Paula.

"No, the United States," was the reply. Sister was quiet for a moment. Then the answer came:

"Yes, yes, Mother Thecla. I will go willingly, whenever and wherever you wish." There were tears in her clear blue eyes, but the words were utterly sincere.

It was the year 1932. Pioneer Paulines left for Argentina, then Brazil. At last, twenty-three-year-old Sister Paula and her companions took the ship bound for America. She heard people mumbling about hard times, about depression years. What could it mean in a rich and powerful nation like America?

The ship reached New York harbor on a sultry June 29th. A figure in black stood on the deck watching the panorama of stately buildings slide by. "We're here," the sister kept repeating to herself. "We're really here. Oh, St. Paul," she prayed, "help me, teach me how to be an apostle like you. One thing I promise," she whispered as the breeze bathed her face with fine ocean spray, "I promise to be loyal to my Congregation, to Father Alberione, to Mother Thecla, for all my life. I would rather die than betray the trust they have given me."

* * * * * * * * * *

The beginnings were hard. The sisters' first convent was a humid third floor apartment crawling with cockroaches. The skimpy meals and strange language were obstacles, too, not to mention a pace far removed from the simple life the sisters had known.

The first Daughters of St. Paul arrived in the United States on June 29, 1932.

"You are not wanted and your apostolate is not needed here," Mother Paula was told. She worried and prayed through anxious days, weeks and months. The community walked one afternoon to St. Patrick's Cathedral. Mother Paula made her way with determination up the side aisle into the sanctuary and placed a medal behind the empty chair of good Cardinal Hayes. She knelt at the communion rail and prayed: "Father Paul, help us now. Prove that you are our father. We were sent to the United States to bring God's word to this great land. Mother Thecla wants us here. It *is* God's will. Open the way. Give us the chance to stay, to grow and prove what our mission can do." She lingered for a few minutes and quickly dried her tears so that the others wouldn't notice.

Official permission to remain came from the Archdiocese of New York in 1934.

Mother Thecla waited anxiously for Pauline letters with distant post marks. She loved to read of the progress of the Congregation in the "mission" lands. United States Paulines saw the 1930's slip off the calendar. The homemade books they had brought from Italy, a little mildewed and yellow, had found their way into the hands of readers. The sisters scrimped and saved for the day when they would have their very own chapel, convent and press room. But how could it be?

"Be satisfied with everything," Mother Paula once said. "We Daughters of St. Paul don't want fancy things. We are poor like Jesus, Mary and Joseph." They were a small and insignificant group but God was watching over them. He proved it by sending American girls to join them. In 1938 the sisters were given the opportunity to buy the old Benziger estate on Staten Island. To Mother Paula it looked like a palace. She walked through the house and began to plan. "This room can be used for the shipping department, and the folding machine can go there, and the cutter, let me see...." It was unbelievable. She wrote to Mother Thecla and asked permission to make the purchase. The answer was "yes."

"It is ours," Mother Paula wrote to Mother General. "It is really ours. We Daughters of St. Paul actually own a home of our own. Now, we have room to prepare the books that we will take to souls." The cellar somehow changed into a bindery, and on a cement pedestal, a stately statue of St. Paul stood. After all, the victory was really his.

A Time To Tremble

Mother Thecla walked back and forth, alongside the hedges, her thoughts keeping time with the rhythm of her steps. The beads slipped through her hands, representing the prayers that were always on her lips.

"It seems like only yesterday we were fighting to end a world war," Mother Thecla was telling our Lord in her confidential way. "That war was to have settled things once and for all. We desire peace so much, and yet, it can never come by war. Oh dear Jesus, peace of heart is found in You alone. When will we learn? This is our task—to bring all men the news of Your true and lasting peace."

The world saw a problem mushroom into a terrible thing; history books call it the Second World War. Dictators rose and fell; power swung this way and that—while good people everywhere trembled and prayed. The positive march of divine and human progress seemed almost at a standstill.

Mother Thecla's dark eyes reflected worry as the war years brought sufferings of every kind. Life was a nightmare of death, bombings, hunger, thirst, poverty and disease. This woman, still so

The war years brought sufferings of every kind.

young, carried the Congregation's problems in her strong, generous heart. There was the food problem, the threat of tuberculosis and other illnesses, the worry for Pauline sisters around the world, and no contact with them possible, and concern for the families of the sisters. Were they alive, well, in need? Down in the air-raid shelter Mother Thecla stared at the ceiling throughout the longest nights in the world.

"My Jesus, give us courage to never lose heart; restore peace. Help us. Help us."

Would it never end? There were moments when a person could wonder. As the noise of artillery fire and small explosions shook their underground room, the Mother General walked among her sisters, serene, thumbing that ever-present rosary. Then she knelt down on the clammy ground. Everything was quiet. Mother Thecla seemed to relax, but the tears that ran down her cheeks told another story. Worries crowded in on her; worries that became *faces* of Pauline sisters who had gone home to be with their families for safety reasons; *faces* of missionaries in other lands suffering in one way or another from the war; *faces* of the very ill Pauline sisters in city hospitals; *faces* of the men, women and children, hungry and sick, who had been knocking daily at the convent door. "Faith," she whispered to herself, "faith, and some day in heaven we will know only joy."

Streaks of yellow came through the spaces in the walls of their underground shelter. The long night was finally over. A voice inside seemed to tell the tired sisters: "For those who trust God the morning will always come."

Gift in a Boxcar

In Staten Island, USA, the mailman moved with steady pace. The route seldom became dull during the war years; so much depended on just a single letter. Many waited at their doors—mothers, fathers, grandparents, young wives, fiancées. The Paulines, too, answered his ring with anxious step. Sister opened the convent door of 78 Fort Place on Staten Island.

"Mailman," the voice said.

"Thank you, God bless you," she replied. Mother Paula took the small bundle and pulled off the string. A letter from Italy caught her eye. It was from her brother, Father David. A brief note, penned with frank simplicity, stated the needs of the war-stricken Paulines, especially for flour.

"Where would you go," asked Mother Paula of a benefactor, "if you wanted to buy a lot of flour?"

"How much is a lot, Sister?"

"Enough to last a large group of people for an entire winter."

"Well, I guess that I would go to Ohio where they grow the wheat." To Ohio Mother Paula would go.

The train pulled out of Penn Station in Manhattan at 9:30 in the morning. Mother Paula waved to the sisters on the platform as the train sped down the track. Ten hours later it chugged into the Erie Street station off Federal Street. The city? Youngstown, Ohio. Four Daughters of St. Paul greeted the tired sister and took her home. Mother Paula unfolded the reasons for her hasty trip. The next morning the sisters gathered for Mass, Holy Communion, meditation. How they prayed that "operation flour" would be a success. After breakfast, Mother Paula and one of the sisters set to work.

The car moved through the nearly empty streets, out of the city, and onto the highway. The pink glow of the steel mills became background as acres of farmland filled the view. Mother Paula glanced at the piece of paper in her hand. It had a name and address and directions written on it. They turned off the highway and followed a narrow, bumpy road. Dust almost hid the car from view.

"There it is," Mother Paula said to the sister-driver, pointing to the farmhouse on the left. A man in overalls came to meet them.

"Mornin'," he said simply, touching the brim of his battered straw hat. "What brings you our way so early?"

"Good morning," came the reply. "We have come to buy wheat."

"You have, huh? How much?"

"Enough to fill a boxcar," she said casually.

The farmer squinted his eyes and stared a full minute. "You're serious, aren't ya?"

"Very serious," sister replied. "A man in Youngstown recommended you. He felt sure that you would give us the best possible price because the flour is for the war victims. Our sisters will be so grateful and we know that God will repay your great sacrifice."

"That's all that counts, Sister," the man said with a grin, "and I sure can use those prayers, too. Now, let's get down to business! I've got the wheat, as much as you want, at a price you can afford. My friend owns a mill. Come inside and we'll call him. Then, we'll need hundred pound sacks to put the flour in. Another company here in the area can donate the sacks. We'll ask them...er, I mean, you can ask them. Who could say 'no' to you?"

The hours passed. By late afternoon the wheat had been ground into flour that filled all the sacks. The sacks were loaded in a large truck and taken back to Youngstown. Meanwhile, Mother Paula had gone on ahead. She was arranging the final link in the chain.

The man behind the grill in the train station could hardly believe his ears. The nun was so earnest, so down-to-earth; she explained about the flour that was on its way. "If you can just transport it 'gratis' to New York City, the National Catholic Relief Services will ship it abroad."

GIFT IN A BOXCAR

"I'll ask the boss, Sister," the man said as he ran his fingers through his hair. "How much flour will you have?"

"Two hundred sacks weighing one hundred pounds each." The man's mouth dropped open. He turned from the window and walked into the office muttering, "The boss will never believe it. He can come out himself and talk to you."

Mother Paula's rosary beads worked overtime as she waited for the verdict. The minutes seemed like eternity.

"Sister," a voice called, as heavy footsteps sounded across the waiting room. He was a tall, red-faced man, a shade too thin, and very businesslike.

"Sister," he began again, "it has always been the policy of this railroad...." He tried to continue: "Situations of this nature are always...we never permit...we know you understand...." Mother Paula's imagination pictured the truck filled with flour. This was the final step.

"If we can get those sacks to New York," she said, "the National Catholic Relief Services will take over from there."

"We never make exceptions," the man said, shaking his head.

"And you will have the prayers of all of our sisters," she continued.

"Prayers?" he asked. "God knows I could use them." He hesitated.

"How much room will you need?" he asked feebly.

"A boxcar."

"A boxcar? Why don't you take a whole train!" he bellowed, throwing his hands in the air.

"You know, Sister, I came out here to tell you 'no.' I guess I didn't say it right. Call me when the load comes in. We'll ship it anywhere you want it to go."

"God bless you," Mother Paula called, as the man went through the door and out of sight.

* * * * * * * * * *

The flour was shipped to Italy, and sometime later...

The huge army truck crawled up the Italian hill. The noise of its powerful engine attracted more than a little attention. Two American soldiers jumped out of the cab and opened the heavy steel doors. By this time the sisters had come outside to witness the whole event. Mother Thecla was there, too. She stood in silence and stared, not knowing what to expect. Slowly the doors opened. It was flour, a whole trailer full.

"From America," the soldiers replied, "from your sisters there." The Mother General stared at what seemed impossible. She came closer, reached up and touched a sack. It was really true! She turned and smiled; the tears in her eyes spoke of her gratitude and joy.

"I have good daughters in America," she said, "yes, good because they are faithful daughters. This is everything; this is everything." She turned to the soldiers: "Come, pay a visit to our chapel, and then we will give you a nice hot lunch."

Mother Thecla would later say that in every Pauline convent she visited, she found something —food, furniture, or other goods—sent by the Daughters of St. Paul of the United States. She often remarked, too, about the generosity of the American people who, by their prayers and offerings, helped the Pauline pioneers.

Wartime Christmas

The baby, so life-like, resting on a pile of straw, seemed to reach out its little arms. What better way to welcome the onlookers who often clustered around the manger scene? Mother Thecla slipped into chapel and gazed at the sight. She glanced to her right and to her left; she was alone in prayer. Soon enough the lights in the chapel flicked on. Someone lit the candles as the entire community filed in. There wasn't a war big enough to cancel midnight Mass. Women's voices filled the chapel with the news of the birth of the King. The choir sang the ancient words of Psalm 2: "The Lord said to me, 'You are my Son; this day have I begotten you....' " Then the Gloria, first chanted by angels some two thousand years before, rang out: *"Glory to God in the highest, and peace on earth to men of good will."* It was a song of success. For when humanity puts God, and the ways of God, before all personal gain, then the result is peace, peace in each heart, and peace among all men.

"The Lord be with you," said the priest.
"And also with you," the altar-boy seminarian answered.

WARTIME CHRISTMAS 77

"A reading from the holy Gospel according to St. Luke." The words filled the chapel with the most incredible story ever written:

"At that time Caesar Augustus published a decree ordering a census of the whole world, and all went to register, each to his own town. Joseph also went from the town of Nazareth in Galilee to Judea to the town of David, there to register with Mary, his espoused wife, who was with child. But while they were there the time came for the child to be born, and she gave birth to her firstborn Son, and wrapped him in swaddling clothes, and laid him in a manger because there was no room for them in the inn." The reading continued, and no one tired of listening.

Mother Thecla was meditating about the first Christmas. She put herself in the place of the shepherds, those nameless, privileged men who had found God in a stable two centuries before.

"We, too, must have faith," Mother Thecla reflected. "And we have to be smart, too. When the shepherds heard about Jesus they forgot everything else, and even though it was the middle of the night, they went to find Him. That is what we all must do: see Jesus, find Jesus, no matter what comes our way."

The sisters left chapel and gathered around Mother Thecla. She was serene and cheerful. She "wore" calmness so well that it had become for her a way of life. Her smile was warm as her gaze scanned the growing community. Any one who knew her well could easily see the worries that were hidden in her eyes. But a mother doesn't share her troubles with her children. She covers them with a smile, with self-giving, with love. This was Mother Thecla.

"Well," she began, "it is Christmas." She folded her hands at her waist and thought for a moment, then added, "Thank God that the bombings have stopped. We no longer hear explosions and gunfire throughout days and nights. Complete peace has not come yet, I know, but if peace is missing for our country and for the world, no one can steal the peace that Jesus brings us: 'peace to men of good will.'

"Do you want to enjoy this peace? Do you want to be numbered among the men of good will? Let us seek to conform ourselves always and in everything to His divine will. If we do this we will be happy on this poor earth, and what is more, we will find heaven in the next.

"Yes, Sisters, it is a wartime Christmas. So let us spend it in fervent prayer, in joy, yes, but also in holy sorrow at the thought of many people suffering, and in prayer for all of them. Let us share deeply the sorrows of the world."

The sisters gathered around the Christmas crib and a spontaneous choir of voices filled the chapel. "Silent night; holy night. All is calm; all is bright...."

If Only a Package Could Talk

He elbowed his way systematically through the crowd that flocked St. Peter's in Rome.

"Sisters," he called to two Daughters of St. Paul. The nuns turned around to see a youthful American soldier coming toward them. He introduced himself, sputtering his best Italian.

"My name is Messina," he said simply, "and I have a sister in your Order back in the United States, on Staten Island." He went to the convent to meet Mother Thecla. While he waited in the parlor, Diego Messina found a book and flipped to a page here and there. He tapped his foot on the floor and glanced up every time he heard the least noise.

Mother Thecla walked down the hall toward the parlor; her mind moved faster than her footsteps. War had broken all communications with the Pauline sisters overseas. No mail could cross the ocean unless it was sent by the military. And at that moment a soldier, a relative of the Congregation, was sitting in the parlor. "Perhaps the boy will send a letter for us," she thought. "At least the sisters in America will know that we are alive and well. And we want to show our love for them, and our concern for their spiritual good. Would I dare? But, of course, why not? When will another chance come?... Maybe not for months. I will give this soldier *the book* to send to Mother Paula, too," she said emphatically.

Diego Messina never realized the "behind-the-scenes" drama that had taken place in Mother Thecla's mind before she stepped into the parlor that day. The soldier was more concerned about the protocol required when meeting a Mother General. But his worries disappeared the minute he saw her.

The sister who stood in the doorway was in her early fifties. A few wrinkles had worked their way around her eyes, and anyone could imagine that in better years her cheeks had been a healthy red. Worry and responsibility had taken heavy tolls on her health, yet they also brought rich reward in virtue and wisdom. Mother Thecla was willing to pay the price, to bear the worry and responsibility of her office, because she really believed it was God's will.

Mother Thecla introduced herself to the soldier. He extended his hand and shook hers vigorously. They exchanged questions and answers, and then the sister said: "No civilian mail can be sent abroad except by the military. I have a little book more precious to the Paulines than you can ever imagine. Will you send it to America, to Mother Paula and the sisters?"

"Sure," the American soldier answered quickly.

Mother Thecla went to get it. "You must take very good care of this," she said as she handed it to him. "Do not show it to anyone, and please, make sure that it gets to its destination. I trust you and I am counting on you."

The soldier did the favor, and sometime later a small, unimportant package arrived at 78 Fort Place on Staten Island. It certainly received a lot of attention. It was postmarked "Italy." The handwritten label bore unfamiliar handwriting, yet could it be from Mother Thecla? Mother Paula untied the string and took off the wrapping which was a plain brown paper bag. The whole thing was quite bewildering. She pulled out a small, black hard cover book, about four inches high and 3/4 of an inch thick. She read the title to herself and then formed the words slowly on her lips. "It is the Constitutions of the Daughters of St. Paul, our holy rule," she said. Tears slid down her cheeks as she opened beyond the title page to read the Pope's approval of their Congregation. She went to chapel, clutching the treasure, and whispered her gratitude to the silent Dweller in the tabernacle. Her memory spun back to the beginnings, so humble and hidden, back to Piedmont, where a handful of young women had announced that with prayer and hard work they would bring Christ to the world with the press. Now had come first papal approval of the Congregation and its rule.

She thought of Mother Thecla, that valiant leader who had given her whole self to the new Congregation. How she longed to see her, if just for a minute or two, to offer congratulations. But, for now, a war was still in the way.

Do You Believe in Miracles?

"Mother Paula, I don't want to have to tell you this, but the high seas have not yet been declared officially safe for passenger travel," the United States government representative said.

"But the war has been over for months now, and I must get to Italy to see the needs of our sisters first hand," the nun answered.

"There isn't any way that I know of," the clerk said apologetically, "no *ordinary* way, that is." Mother Paula thought for a moment.

"Will you do me one favor, then?" she asked. Her face reflected that perpetual belief in the goodness of her fellowmen.

"Don't tell me, Sister. I'll bet I can guess. You want me to perform a miracle, right?"

"Right," she laughed. "Can you call your commander and ask him?"

"The Colonel?" the clerk asked weakly. "He won't like it, Sister."

Mother Paula smiled and said, "you promised that you would help, if possible. It is possible to at least ask, right?"

"True," the man said. "All right, Mother Paula. You pray and I'll talk to the Colonel." She showed him the rosary she had pressed in the palm of her hand. "I *have* been praying all the while," she assured him. "But now we will re-double our efforts."

The red-faced clerk dialed each digit carefully. His expression changed from hesitation to determination and back. "Pray hard," he whispered as the phone rang. The receiver clicked on the other end. Connections were made and in seconds the Colonel was on the line.

"The sisters want permission to sail to Italy," the clerk began, trying to sound convincing. "They must get there as soon as possible. I know what you're going to tell me. The waters are still unsafe, but, what can I say, the sisters believe in miracles!"

There was silence for a minute. "I believe in miracles, too, as a matter of fact," the Colonel retorted. "But I don't know if Washington does, so I'll have to clear with them before any permission is issued. Hold on." He was amazingly calm as he picked up another phone and dialed. When Washington answered, he briefed the unnamed voice on the other end, stating the reason for the call. The answer came quickly.

"This afternoon an official bulletin will be released declaring that the waters are now safe for civilian travel. You will be getting the news shortly."

"That is all I have to know," the Colonel replied. "This information is going to make some sisters very happy." He hung up the phone and picked up the receiver to relay the message to the clerk.

"Tell the sisters that they have every permission to sail," the Colonel said. "And it is official. They certainly have Someone pulling for them, don't they?"

"Sisters," the clerk mumbled, "you probably expected this, but...for me it is incredible. The way is clear. You are free to sail." His eyes seemed a bit more shiny than usual.

* * * * * * * * * *

The Italian freighter churned through the blue Atlantic on the familiar route to Italy. Mother Paula stood on the deck and gazed at the statue of liberty. She remembered another day, fourteen years before, when the ship she was on was coming into the harbor instead of going out. She recalled the fears, the struggles, the utter amazement she had felt when looking at the magnificent city of New York for the first time. She and her companions knew *no* English and *no*body except Father Francis Borrano, of the Society of St. Paul, who had come to the pier to welcome them.

It had been 1932, a depression year, and some New York authorities had suggested that the sisters go back to where they had come from, but twenty-three-year-old Sister Paula had been told by Father Alberione and Mother Thecla to plant the Pauline dream in the great land of America. And she stayed, despite many difficulties, because she really believed that this was God's will. Many tears, prayers and worries had filled those fourteen years, but the way now was steady and sure.

Mother Paula watched the New York skyline grow smaller and smaller and felt the lump grow in her throat. She would only be gone for a while. But how she would miss the budding province. Then came the full realization that, for her, America had become "home."

Sixteen days later...the armed forces patrolling Naples tried to tell Mother Thecla that none of her Pauline sisters could possibly be on the freighter. But she wouldn't leave.

"Look, Sister," a guard suggested, "why don't you go back to the convent where you will be much more comfortable and if your sisters arrive today we will let you know."

"Oh, no," Mother Thecla said kindly but firmly, "I prefer to wait."

"What's she doing here?" a uniformed officer asked.

"Thinks her sisters are coming in on a ship" came the reply. "Impossible, I know, but she says they're there and that's it!"

* * * * * * * * * *

The ship seemed to take forever to pull into port. On deck, Mother Paula and the first novices of the American province clung to the rail, their eyes glued to the Neopolitan coastline. It took time and far too much protocol but at last the sisters walked down the gangplank onto Italian soil. Mother Thecla was waiting there.

Promises Must Be Kept

During Mother Paula's stay in Italy, an unusual event took place.

A small car pulled out of the convent driveway. The two sisters in the front seat said the rosary aloud as they drove through narrow streets. Minutes later they pulled up alongside a large stone building easily identifiable as a city hospital.

"Why are you taking me here?" Mother Paula asked Mother Thecla.

"There is someone I want you to see," answered the other. They walked through the grey halls toward their destination. Mother Thecla led the way. She knocked lightly on a door and entered the room.

"Sister Jesualda," she said, embracing the patient, "today I have a special surprise. I have brought Mother Paula from America to meet you." And turning to the visitor she explained:

"Sister Jesualda is confined to city hospital with tuberculosis; she has been here, away from her convent, for six years." Mother Paula shook her head in disbelief. She gulped down the tears and murmured: "Something has to be done." The three sisters prayed, talked and laughed for a little while. Then, it was time to leave.

"We will be back tomorrow," Mother Thecla promised.

The car pulled out into the street. This time it moved to the edge of the city and climbed into the peaceful Albano hills on the outskirts of Rome.

"Pull over here," Mother Thecla directed. Mother Paula stopped the car and they got out.

"What do you think of it?" asked the Mother General.

"The view is beautiful," answered the other.

"Remember Sister Jesualda?" continued Mother Thecla. "Well, she is part of my plan. I wanted you to see her, and I wanted you to see the property where we can and must build a hospital, a very unique hospital for our own sick religious and for all sisters of any congregation who are temporarily or incurably ill. This hospital will be equipped with whatever is needed to make a body whole and well again, and it will also care for the continued spiritual growth of the sisters so that pain, suffering and even fear will draw them closer to God, and to the great heights of union with Jesus and Mary to which they, as spouses of Christ, are called."

Mother Paula nodded her head in agreement. "And," she said, "we Daughters of St. Paul from the States will pay for the land."

Mother General glowed with joy. "I knew you would," she said.

The car retraced its way back through the streets of Rome enroute to the Pauline convent.

"You will be going to America soon," Mother Thecla mused. "We will miss you here."

* * * * * * * * * *

The freighter set out for America with only one Daughter of St. Paul on board. The sister smiled and waved at the large group of Pauline sisters who had come to say good-bye. The novices she had brought to Rome would stay on for the special year of novitiate formation. But for Mother Paula it was time to go home.

"I wanted you to see the property where we can and must build a hospital," Mother Thecla said.

Growing Pains

The war was over, and the Daughters of St. Paul looked for new avenues to open to their apostolate of bringing the Word of God to men.

"Soon you will be all over the world," spoke Father Alberione to the Pauline co-foundress, Mother Thecla.

"But, how?" she wanted to ask. And yet she had never questioned this remarkable man, because whatever he had said, since the start in 1915, had proved true.

Mother Thecla recalled their rapid growth throughout Italy, and then the expansion to Argentina and Brazil in 1931; to the United States in 1932; to the Philippines in 1938. Could there still be more growing to do? The sister went to chapel and asked the Divine Master to open her eyes to see the possibilities of further expansion. And the inspiration came.

Daughters of St. Paul, in twos and fours, left during the post-war years for Switzerland in 1946, for Chile, Japan, Colombia and Mexico in 1948, for India in 1950, Canada in 1952, England and Australia in 1955, Spain and Venezuela in 1956, Portugal in 1957, the Congo in 1958, Formosa in 1959, Peru and Korea in 1960, Malaysia in 1961,

Bolivia in 1963 and Germany, Uruguay, Uganda and Nigeria in 1964. As the Congregation planted its roots around the world the pioneer Pauline sisters relived lean beginnings and many recalled first-hand a poverty similar to the early years.

"It is good to struggle," Father Alberione would remind in his fatherly way. "It is good to have bills. That gives us the incentive to work and to work hard."

Mother Thecla watched over the Congregation that could now be called "world-wide." She was the inspiration behind the Pauline religious life and the apostolate. Her spirit pulsed in the veins of the sisters around the world, who in turn taught the postulants, or beginners, who would become the Congregation of tomorrow.

The aging Mother General scanned a large world map that represented humanity on its way to God. Her heart filled with joy to think that Daughters of St. Paul were printing and diffusing books in the major languages of every continent. They had begun to broadcast daily in radio stations in several countries. They had long before begun producing films in Italy; they were moving into television; they were putting out uplifting record albums. The Pauline apostles were to make God known through every page of a book that came from their presses, from the pamphlet or leaflet that was carried personally to men of every race and creed. They were to make the world

God-centered by turning the powerful opinion-makers—the press, radio, television and motion pictures—into tools at work for man's salvation.

"Your apostolate," spoke the Founder, "is as old as the Gospel and as new as the most up-to-date instrument of communication invented by modern man."

Mother Thecla saw the faces of her sisters around the world. Now they represented every race and culture, praying, working and sharing their way of life. It thrilled and humbled her.

"I think of you and pray for you so often," she wrote to a sister. "Even though we cannot see each other we can meet at the tabernacle. Pray much; pray well and increase your desire to become a great saint."

"When you see the moon on a bright clear night," she told others with a twinkle in her eyes, "remember that even though I will be far away I will be thinking of you and praying for you."

* * * * * * * * *

Mother Thecla's weekly letters to her convents around the world helped to preserve the unity she knew to be so important for the growing Congregation.

The Queen of Apostles shrine built by Father Alberione after the Second World War with the help of Pauline priests, brothers and sisters, was completed, and the hospital for religious, with the same name, was completed in 1949.

Growth...expansion...so vital to the work of God—but how was all this possible?

Mother Thecla knew. How many times daily she repeated the formula of the Founder:

"By myself I can do nothing, but with God I can do all things. For the love of God I want to do all things. To Him honor and glory. To me, the eternal reward."

She Gave All She Had

Frequent trips to convents all over the world by ship and later by jet, countless hours of prayer, work, and continual dedication to the sisters, her daughters in Christ—all of this was bound to take its toll on the health of Mother Thecla.

Her pen moved carefully across the stationery. It wrote strange words: "Tomorrow, the Feast of the Most Holy Trinity, I want to offer my life that the Daughters of St. Paul may all become saints." It was May 27, 1961.

"I have spent all my life for the Congregation," she whispered to herself. "Can I not offer my death too? I know that it is not far away, but how can I be afraid? Death is the only door that can open heaven to me. It will open the door to Jesus. And what more can a religious desire than to possess Jesus? With Him I feel strong, generous, desirous of becoming holy. I want to do everything for Him, for heaven. Everything temporary has no value."

To the sisters who gathered for Sunday conference, the ailing sister spoke words of unforgettable worth. "It is hard to become saints," she said, "but we don't want to give up the idea for that. Let us work steadily, with faith, and in the best way we know how. God sees. God is a good cameraman, and at the judgment He will project the film. See to it that you are good stars—shining stars!"

By February of 1963 Mother Thecla was ill enough to mention it, which was most unusual for her. "You know," she said with that curious grin, "I do not feel well! I'm not sick enough to stay in bed though, so I must go on, even with the pain and suffering. I feel truly that all is not well, but...whatever God wants."

The novices who clustered around Mother Thecla as she walked with them out on the grounds chattered happily about their dreams and goals. They recounted stories of the apostolate with all their youthful enthusiasm. Suddenly, the laughter ceased and the circle of young faces became serious. They saw the face of their beloved Mother General grow twisted with pain as she struggled to say words that remained only sounds. They took her inside and put her to bed. Anxious sisters hovered over her, fearing the worst. She received the sacrament of the sick. So still as to barely seem to breathe, Mother Thecla hung on to life; five hours later she opened her eyes and tried to speak. After a few days the crisis passed, but her health had been gravely impaired. Mother Thecla was taken to the Queen of Apostles hospital to recover.

There was more time to pray and think of God now and the sister who so loved solitude

"God is a good cameraman, and at the judgment He will project the film. See to it that you are good stars—shining stars!"

The novices who clustered around
Mother Thecla chattered happily about
their dreams and goals.

knew how to make the most of her time. As the days passed, Mother Thecla began to get up from bed for short intervals. How she loved to go out onto the veranda and look out into the warm starry nights. God was so near. One night she looked up at the stars; her gaze roamed the heavens.

"There," she pointed, as the words formed slowly on her lips, "there beyond those stars is our Father's house, the house of the Father, who is waiting for us. How beautiful it must be to go home...."

We Must All Be "Builders"

Mother Thecla, alone in her hospital room, worked her way slowly out of bed and found a scrap of paper and pencil. She tried to write. Even though her mind was lucid, her hand could produce only an unintelligible scribble. Shame filled her and a large tear rolled down her cheek. She crumpled up the piece of paper and hid it. Later, when the sisters came in she unraveled it and showed it to them. One of the sisters squeezed the Mother General's hands and whispered, "It takes time to get well, just a little more time."

"I am no longer able to govern the Congregation," Mother Thecla managed to say. "It is necessary that I resign, and that another superior be elected."

The sisters who gathered around shook their heads in a definite refusal. She retained her position without mentioning the subject again.

The chaplain of the Albano hospital sat by her bedside and listened as Mother Thecla confided worries that wouldn't give her a moment's rest.

"I am not doing any penance," she said sadly, "I can't even do any work. Tell me what I should do, what mortification I should make."

"Accept this penance," the priest said slowly. "Accept with patience your inability to attend to the duties of your office, the renunciation of activity, the confinement to apparent idleness. This is your penance. To conform yourself to the will of God, this is the best penance you can do."

The Mother General nodded her head. He was right.

* * * * * * * * *

Days passed. Mother Thecla sat in her chair near the window and watched the construction men building the Albano hospital's new wing. She thought back to the day when she had chosen the land, and even farther back, to the war days and nights, many of which had been spent in the air-raid shelter. She had determined then to build that hospital for religious. And now, in 1963, a new addition was being added.

"God is good," she thought to herself. Her eyes followed the muddy boots of the industrious men who hoisted beams and mixed cement. When the work looked dangerous or very difficult she would whisper "Hail Marys" that all would go well and especially that our Lady would make their burden light.

WE MUST ALL BE "BUILDERS"

The hospital wing continued to take shape. Its progress seemed to have special meaning for the ailing Mother General. She, who had spent her lifetime "building" a strong Congregation, not with steel and bricks but with faith, humility and obedience, could not be defeated now that the "external" part of her mission was done. She would continue to "build" the shrine of sanctity within her own heart until the end of her life.

In the Footsteps of the Suffering Christ

The picture at the foot of the bed seemed to come alive to the sick sister who stared at the wall where it hung. The head of Christ, wrapped in thorns, reflected with vivid lines His agony and pain. Mother Thecla loved the picture. She hoisted herself up to a semi-sitting position and thought: "I have worked all my life. Now God is asking me to suffer. Together with action, suffering is needed because Jesus Himself first worked and then suffered in life. I want to follow You, Jesus," she whispered softly to the picture on the wall. "I want to imitate You. Now, to what little work I have done I add suffering. As a religious I gave myself to You. Now would I refuse to follow You to Calvary?"

"How do you feel, Mother?" the sister-nurse asked anxiously.

"As Jesus wants," came the reply. "We all are in God's hands."

February 5, 1964 dawned grey and cold. The morning passed. Father Alberione came to visit Mother Thecla briefly to bless and encourage her.

Just before noon Mother Ignatius, her Vicar, went to the sickroom to say that she had to go to the airport and would be out for a few hours. Then she walked to the door and turned to see the Mother General gesturing her back. Sister stopped. An unusual feeling seemed to speed through her veins. Her feet moved almost mechanically back to the bedside of her foundress. She instinctively bent over and Mother Thecla, slowly, deliberately, traced with her thumb a cross on sister's forehead. Then, she embraced and kissed the sister who would become the second Mother General of the Daughters of St. Paul. With these gestures she handed over a Congregation of women religious, numbering two thousand, in twenty-eight nations, to Mother Ignatius Balla, the sister of her choice. Everything was complete.

At 12:30 A.M. her agony began.

Home...Beyond Those Stars

"She dies for the Congregation," a sister whispered. "She dies for all of us. This agony, all this pain, is offered willingly for her daughters. She is 'buying' courage and fidelity so that we Pauline sisters will remain strong, firm, united. Oh, if I could only take a little of the pain from her. But she would never let me. She was always like that...."

The fever mounted. Mother Thecla's face became twisted with anguish, her body jolted by cruel spasms. The pages of her memory seemed to spin like loose-leaf sheets in a November wind, and the events of her life passed in front of her. She was a little girl again back in Castagnito.

"Mama," she was asking as they walked along, "what will it be like to receive Jesus in Holy Communion?"

"It will be like going to heaven," came the sure reply.

"Will I go to heaven soon?"

"Oh no, only after a lifetime of hard work."

"What kind of work? Sewing, cooking?"

"Perhaps, but the kind doesn't matter. What matters is to do what you can, the best way you can, for love of God."

HOME...BEYOND THOSE STARS

The pages began to spin once more. She was a teenager again. "What do you have to do?" Mama Vincenza was asking after meeting Father Alberione.

"Just obey him."

Time jumped ahead. The carriage was bouncing swiftly down the road.

"Good-bye, Mama, Papa, John, Costanzo, Charles. Good-bye, Castagnito."

The voice of Father Alberione sounded out of the past: "Bishop Castelli has asked me if you and your companions will take charge of his diocesan newspaper. Shall I accept for you?" Fifteen days later saw the first issue of "Valsusa." From then on growth of the Pauline dream—vows, the move to Rome, countless prayers to St. Paul, father of the infant Congregation, but not without worry; the sacrifices, hard on the body but good for the soul; criticism; suffering. God's will...God's will, no matter the cost. Advances in the apostolate, miracles of faith. No human means could explain them.

"Just obey," spoke Father Alberione, "and you will see. Obey.... Obey.... Obedience works miracles."

Approval of the Constitutions, first diocesan and then Papal approval. "Our way is now certain," spoke the Founder. "The Church has put her stamp of final approval on your apostolate. You are sure of being in the will of God."

Sisters walking in pairs, carrying leather bags filled with books, sisters staffing St. Paul book and film centers, sisters working the machines that produce books, radio and television programs, films and the other media. Sisters of every background and culture, laboring for God and people. Her voice sounded: "And to think, we used to be nine; we used to be nine."

Then the Mother General's body became still. She seemed scarcely to breathe.

Prayers led by Father Alberione filled the sick-room where a foundress lay dying. Soon, all was quiet. It was February 5, 1964. Mother Thecla's life on this earth was over; she had found eternal life.

"Look to heaven," she tells our modern age. "Up there all human pains vanish; miseries disappear. We will be perfect, is it not so? Oh, to rise again, young, beautiful, in the fullness of strength. To rise never again to suffer, never again to die!

"Look up to heaven, not downwards to earth, because here below we will always find something that is not right. Look up at the clear blue sky.... Let us push ourselves ever upward—all the way to heaven!

"That must be our joy and the thought of heaven must fill us with the courage to overcome every difficulty. Always look to heaven. Always desire and seek heaven with all our strength, not only for ourselves but for all people."

Mother Thecla Merlo

Daughters of St. Paul

IN MASSACHUSETTS
    50 St. Paul's Ave. Jamaica Plain, Boston, MA 02130; **617-522-8911; 617-522-0875;**
    172 Tremont Street, Boston, MA 02111; **617-426-5464; 617-426-4230**
IN NEW YORK
    78 Fort Place, Staten Island, NY 10301; **212-447-5071**
    59 East 43rd Street, New York, NY 10017; **212-986-7580**

    625 East 187th Street, Bronx, NY 10458; **212-584-0440**
    525 Main Street, Buffalo, NY 14203; **716-847-6044**
IN NEW JERSEY
    Hudson Mall — Route 440 and Communipaw Ave., Jersey City, NJ 07304; **201-433-7740**
IN CONNECTICUT
    202 Fairfield Ave., Bridgeport, CT 06604; **203-335-9913**
IN OHIO
    2105 Ontario St. (at Prospect Ave.), Cleveland, OH 44115; **216-621-9427**
    25 E. Eighth Street, Cincinnati, OH 45202; **513-721-4838**
IN PENNSYLVANIA
    1719 Chestnut Street, Philadelphia, PA 19103; **215-568-2638**
IN FLORIDA
    2700 Biscayne Blvd., Miami, FL 33137; **305-573-1618**
IN LOUISIANA
    4403 Veterans Memorial Blvd., Metairie, LA 70002; **504-887-7631; 504-887-0113**
    1800 South Acadian Thruway, P.O. Box 2028, Baton Rouge, LA 70821 **504-343-4057; 504-343-3814**
IN MISSOURI
    1001 Pine Street (at North 10th), St. Louis, MO 63101; **314-621-0346; 314-231-1034**
IN ILLINOIS
    172 North Michigan Ave., Chicago, IL 60601; **312-346-4228; 312-346-3240**
IN TEXAS
    114 Main Plaza, San Antonio, TX 78205; **512-224-8101**
IN CALIFORNIA
    1570 Fifth Avenue, San Diego, CA 92101; **714-232-1442**
    46 Geary Street, San Francisco, CA 94108; **415-781-5180**
IN HAWAII
    1143 Bishop Street, Honolulu, HI 96813; **808-521-2731**
IN ALASKA
    750 West 5th Avenue, Anchorage AK 99501; **907-272-8183**
IN CANADA
    3022 Dufferin Street, Toronto 395, Ontario, Canada
IN ENGLAND
    128, Notting Hill Gate, London W11 3QG, England
    133 Corporation Street, Birmingham B4 6PH, England
    5A-7 Royal Exchange Square, Glasgow G1 3AH, England
    82 Bold Street, Liverpool L1 4HR, England
IN AUSTRALIA
    58 Abbotsford Rd., Homebush, N.S.W., Sydney 2140, Australia